SUPER
SURPRISING
TRiViA
ABOUT
ARTIFICIAL
INTELLIGENCE

by Lisa M. Bolt Simons

CAPSTONE PRESS
a capstone imprint

Spark is published by Capstone Press, an imprint of Capstone
1710 Roe Crest Drive, North Mankato, Minnesota 56003
capstonepub.com

Library of Congress Cataloging-in-Publication Data is available on the
Library of Congress website.
ISBN: 9781669050292 (hardcover)
ISBN: 9781669071655 (paperback)
ISBN: 9781669050254 (ebook PDF)

Summary: Think you know a lot about robots and artificial intelligence?
Prepare to learn even more about the technology that exists now and the
mind-blowing advances being developed for the future. You'll be surprised
by how much you'll discover in this totally terrific book of trivia about
artificial intelligence.

Editorial Credits
Editor: Mandy Robbins; Designer: Heidi Thompson; Media Researcher:
Jo Miller; Production Specialist: Tori Abraham

Image Credits
Alamy: REUTERS, 10; Getty Images: iLexx, Cover (bottom left), janiecbros,
12, LL28, 13, WANG ZHAO, 24; Newscom/Edwin Remsberg/agefotostock,
7; Shutterstock: AlexLMX, 21, Antonio Guillem, 9, Arlette Lopez, 27, aslysun,
20, BaniHasyim, 15, Billion Photos, 11, Blue Planet Studio, 29 (bottom),
David Cardinez, 8, DisobeyArt, 22, Dmytro Zinkevych, 5, Gorodenkoff, 18,
Have a nice day Photo, Cover (bottom right), Hollygraphic, (design element)
throughout, Laborant, 17, Lukas Gojda, Cover (left), Marko Aliaksandr, 16,
mexrix, (background) throughout, Petair, 19, Phonlamai Photo, Cover (top
right), rozdemir, 28, Ryan DeBerardinis, 23, Sonsedska Yuliia, 25, Studio
Romantic, 29 (top), Suwin, 14, Vantage_DS, 26 (all), Volodymyr Krasyuk,
Cover (top left), Zapp2Photo, 6

Printed and bound in China. PO5379

TABLE OF CONTENTS

Words in **bold** are in the glossary.

MACHINE SMARTS

How much do you know about robots? Some can think like humans and learn over time. They're called artificial intelligence or AI. Robots and other machines have AI. They get smarter every day. Get ready for some surprising AI facts!

AI FEEDING US

AI robots save farmers time. One AI robot uses 24 arms to pick strawberries. It can even check how **ripe** the fruit is!

AI can spot bugs on crops. It sends a message to the farmer's smartphone. Then farmers spray their fields to kill the bugs.

Six-wheeled robots deliver groceries and other goods short distances. They use AI to find safe routes to travel.

Want to keep an eye on your food delivery? AI runs apps that help customers track orders.

You want fries with that? The Flippy 2 robot can help you. It works the fryer station at restaurants. It preps food with its **thermal**, 3D vision.

Time for dessert? A robotic **waterjet** cuts cake in no time!

MEDICAL ADVANCES

Researchers use AI technology to understand **DNA**. This could mean huge advances in medical treatments.

AI is often used in robot-assisted surgeries. Will robots perform surgeries on their own someday?

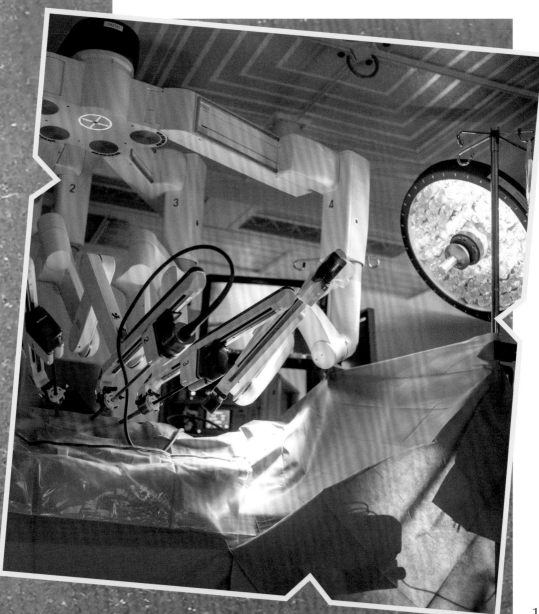

SMART TRANSPORT

Drone taxis are helicopters without pilots. These AI drones may be used in some Asian cities by 2024.

Qatar Airlines has MetaHuman flight attendants on their website. They give visitors a **virtual reality** tour of everything the airline has to offer.

A Vertical Take-Off and Landing is called a VTOL. It can carry packages that weigh more than most people. AI helps it pick up and drop off items quickly without human contact.

Train engines can be driven by AI technology. A human can take over in case of emergencies.

Driverless cars already exist. A person has to sit in the driver's seat, though. They can take over if the AI makes a mistake.

When will driverless cars be common in the United States? It might be as soon as 2030.

In the future, driverless cars will use electricity instead of gasoline.

CLEANUP IN AISLE AI

New vacuum robots use AI to avoid running over pet poop.

AI robots are recycling superheroes. They know the difference between paper, plastic, metal, electronics, and food. They sort them fast!

GLASS   METAL   PAPER   PLASTIC

Half of all ocean pollution is tiny bits of plastic. AI tech in drones can tell the difference between plastic and sea life. They help with cleanup.

A company called Cortexia puts cameras on trucks, cars, buses, and bikes. AI spots where and when trash piles up. Then the garbage trucks are sent out!

AI ANIMALS

AlphaDog is a robot dog. It delivers packages.

It can work as a guide dog too.

A cat shelter in China is controlled by AI. The AI can sense when a cat approaches. Then it opens its door. There cats can find shelter, food, and water.

HOW SMART CAN IT GET?

Which AI **platform** do you think is smarter?

Google Assistant, Siri, or Alexa? If you said Google

Assistant, you're right!

In 2013, AI was about as smart as a four-year-old human. Many experts think it will one day be smarter than adults.

Experts build and program AI tech. But this tech is designed to constantly learn. Sometimes AI makes decisions that its creators don't understand.

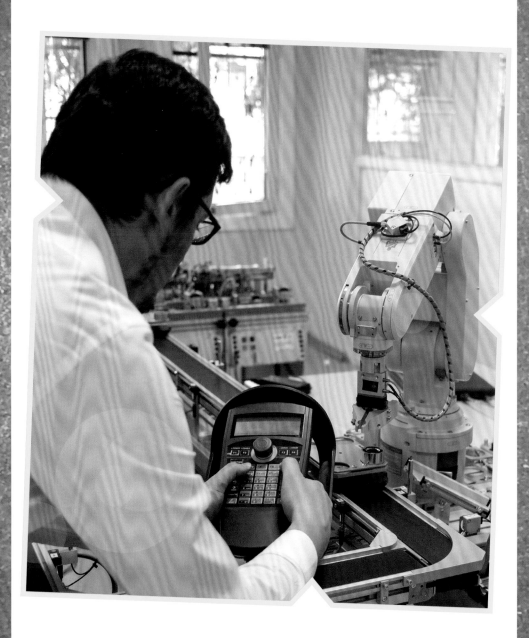

AI could improve dating apps. It might predict who people are attracted to and get along with better than today's tech.

Will humans and AI robots one day fall in love? Some experts think so.

Glossary

DNA (dee-en-AY)—the molecule that carries the genes; found inside the nucleus of cells

drone (DROHN)—an unmanned, remote-controlled aircraft or missile

platform (PLAT-form)—an app or website that serves as a base from which a service is provided

ripe (RYPE)—ready to pick and eat

thermal (THUR-muhl)—having to do with heat or holding in heat

virtual reality (VUHR-choo-uhl ree-AL-uh-tee)—a three-dimensional world created by a computer user where things onscreen seem to come to life

waterjet (WAH-tuhr-jet)—a very high-speed stream of water

Read More

Jackson, Tom. *Artificial Intelligence: When Computers Get Smart!* New York: Kingfisher, 2022.

Klepeis, Alicia Z. *Artificial Intelligence and Work*. North Mankato, MN: An imprint of Capstone Press, 2019.

Mattern, Joanne. *All About Artificial Intelligence.* Lake Elmo, MN: Focus Readers, 2023.

Internet Sites

Agrobot
agrobot.com/e-series

Artificial Intelligence
kids.britannica.com/kids/article/artificial-intelligence/390648

Artificial Intelligence for Kids
create-learn.us/ai-for-kids

Index

About the Author

@Jillian Raye Photography

Lisa M. Bolt Simons has published more than 60 nonfiction children's books and middle grade novels, as well as an adult history title. She's received accolades for both her nonfiction and fiction. Originally from Colorado, she currently resides in a town of 140 in Minnesota. She's a mom to adult girl/boy twins and is a wife to a book-loving guy.